COACHING T-BALL

Organize And Optimize Your
Way To A Great Season

Jerry Baseball

thosearegood LLC

Copyright © 2022 thosearegood LLC

All rights reserved

No part of this book may be reproduced, or stored in a retrieval system, or transmitted in any form or by any means, electronic, mechanical, photocopying, recording, or otherwise, without express written permission of the publisher.

ISBN: 979-8-9856956-1-8

Cover design by: Jerry Baseball
Printed in the United States of America

To Melanie, for signing me up

CONTENTS

Title Page
Copyright
Dedication
Preface
Signup   1
Organization and Recruiting Coaches   2
Equipment   4
Coaching Philosophy   6
Homework   9
Practice   11
The Night Before the Game   15
Gameday   18
Practice Expansion   23
Miscellaneous Issues   26
Victory!   28
About The Author   29
Coaching Youth Baseball   31

PREFACE

Hi, I'm Jerry Baseball, and I was looking for guidance when I set out to coach my oldest son's t-ball team three years ago.

There were some books available, but they were either too expert "read my 300-page book on what I learned during 27 years of coaching t-ball," or too flippant "I coached a season of t-ball and lived to write this book."

So, I experimented with every aspect of coaching a t-ball team. Some of the tactics in this book worked so great the first time that I never had to change them. Certain things I only figured out toward the end of the second season.

Even though I was constantly tweaking things, we still outclassed most opposing teams. And if any team outclassed us, I copied what they were doing either immediately, like putting the lineup card on a huge piece of poster board, or the following season, like getting the biggest coaching staff possible.

So, after coaching two successful seasons of t-ball, one with each of my sons, I wanted to write a template for what I would do if I coached another season.

If you're a frazzled parent, you can read this book in 30 minutes, or if you're crunched for time, listen to the audiobook during your commute, and have a plan to lead you through a great season.

Even if you haven't played baseball since Little League and you're better with spreadsheets than you are with kids, you'll trounce the other coaches by implementing what you learn in this book. People will come up to you mid-season and say things like, "you're so great with kids," and you'll look around to see if a kindergarten teacher is walking by.

So, read this book, follow the plan, and prepare to have people ask, "are you a professional t-ball coach?" My answer is always "I wish!"

SIGNUP

Pre-Signup

Start recruiting assistant coaches now! Most leagues will let you sign up together, so recruit friends to coach with you. If you have to go it alone at this stage, that's ok too. You can recruit coaches later.

Sign Up

Sign up to be a t-ball coach! Either volunteer to coach during your kid's signup or hunt down the commissioner after the fact. The commissioner will be happy you volunteered, and you will be a great coach.

ORGANIZATION AND RECRUITING COACHES

Organization

Use a Team Organization App.

Once you get the roster from the league, add everyone into a team organization app. TeamSnap works well.

Then, add the first practice, and only the first practice, in the app. After adding the first practice, ask everyone to enter their player's availability. Once everyone says whether they are a yes/no/maybe, you'll know everyone can use the app. Follow up with any laggards by text or phone to get them logged into the app.

Once everyone is in the app, only communicate using the app for the rest of the season.

Recruit Coaching Staff

Send out a welcome message in the app chat that is, primarily, a call for coaches. "Hello, parents of the Pottstown Panthers. Welcome to an exciting season. I'm Jerry Baseball, the head coach. We need four additional coaches to run this team. Please message me directly to volunteer."

You want 4-5 coaches minimum. Sometimes, you'll get lucky and have one or two parents that signed up to be assistants through the league. Regardless, more coaches are always better.

For instance, when you're up to bat, you need:

1. A first-base coach
2. A third-base coach
3. A coach at home plate near the tee
4. One or two coaches on the bench to keep the players safe

Once you have enough coaches, add the entire schedule, including practices and games, to the app.

Make sure you wait until you have enough coaches before putting the whole schedule up. Otherwise, someone will think, "I'm going to have to miss the game against the Royals on May 23rd, so I'll let other people else coach." Eliminate the potential for that excuse.

Ask everyone to fill out each player's availability immediately at the beginning of the season for every practice and game. Getting the commitments in early will help the season run smoothly.

Parental Interaction

If you want parents to behave in a certain way, send a message to everyone on the app before the season or games start.

If, for instance, you would like all non-coaching parents to help their kids get to their correct position each inning, message them the night before the game in the app chat.

EQUIPMENT

Bats

As the coach, buy an appropriate bat for your kid and let all the players on the team use it.

For most players, lighter is better for a t-ball bat. Lightweight bats will lead to swings that look better overall.

A bat with a large "drop" is good too. "Drop" is the difference between length in inches and weight in ounces. For example, -12 and -13 are good "drop" measurements for t-ball.

Lastly, when choosing between two light bats with a high drop, choose the bat with a bigger barrel.

Feel free to encourage all players to use the same bat if it's the best one your team has. Some players get caught up in wanting to use "their" bat. For players in love with their heavy bat, let them know that even major leaguers share bats.

Balls

Make sure you're playing with some sort of softer ball. If a hardball makes its way into your ball inventory, throw it out immediately.

The more balls you have, the better. The team can get more reps in practice with more balls. In addition, players can take a ball or two home to practice.

Add some tennis balls and a kickball to your equipment bag.

More balls = More reps = Better team

Helmets

Every offensive player has to wear a helmet in t-ball. Players can get hit with the ball while running or by a teammate swinging the bat while warming up. Wearing a helmet with a mask is a good decision because fielders have poor throwing accuracy, and everyone has slow reaction times.

Pants

It is easy for players to scrape themselves on the infield dirt, so encourage players to wear baseball pants. Many t-ball players will want to wear shorts when it is hot. Send a reminder to parents through the team app recommending pants for safety, even on hot days.

COACHING PHILOSOPHY

Coaching Attitude

Always be positive! "Great job," "looking good," and "nice" are a good start.

Everything good happens because of someone else: a player, an assistant coach, a parent.

Everything bad that happens is your fault.

If the players struggle with a drill in practice, it's your fault for introducing it too soon.

If a player has a hard time hitting the ball in the game, it's your fault for failing to address it last practice. Say, "We will practice that next practice, and then you'll be crushing the ball." Then, practice whichever skill needs work.

Players enjoy seeing an adult take the blame and then making a plan to fix it.

Avoid saying things like "well, they just won't do what they are supposed to do." Other quotes along these lines are "this is painful" and "it's like herding cats." If an assistant coach says things like that, move them to an easier assignment.

Horseplay

Hopefully, on every t-ball team, there are kids that run around like maniacs. They grab a ball and throw it back and forth before practice starts. They always start to do the activity before it's time to do the activity. These are the future superstars. Please tolerate this disruptive behavior as much as possible.

The way to avoid this behavior is to be on time and organized.

If practice starts on time and all the equipment is where it needs to be, there will be less disruptive horseplay.

Horseplay is an indication that you need to be more organized, not that the players need to "focus."

Ready Position?

It is painful to hold "ready position" for longer than a second before the ball is hit. Any baseball players at the high school level or higher are "ready" for about half a second, and they "hop" into their ready position.

Anyone that tells a t-ball player to hold "ready position" for an extended time, even something as "short" as 30 seconds, is exposing themselves as a know-nothing.

In t-ball, focus on having each player face the batter with their hands somewhere in front or to the side of them. Hands clasped behind one's back is dangerous. If you can coach the players to get into "ready position" for the tenth of a second as the ball is being hit, great. If not, don't make the players hold "ready position" for an extended period. No one does that!

Focus And Attention Span

Focus and attention span correlate with ability. There are, of course, laser-focused clumsy players and athletic players with short attention spans. However, they are rare. For the most part, better players pay more attention because people like things they are good at. So, if you would like players to pay more attention, make an effort to improve their skills.

Many parents yell at their kids to "pay attention" in t-ball. "Pay attention" can be summarized as "if you had elite concentration, you could be above average." While true, it's easier to teach a player where the bases are than to hope they have the focus of a pro to go with their novice t-ball skills.

HOMEWORK

Homework

Give your team two homework assignments during the season. Give "Identify The Bases" out at the end of the first practice, and give "Identify The Positions" out at the end of the second practice.

Identify The Bases

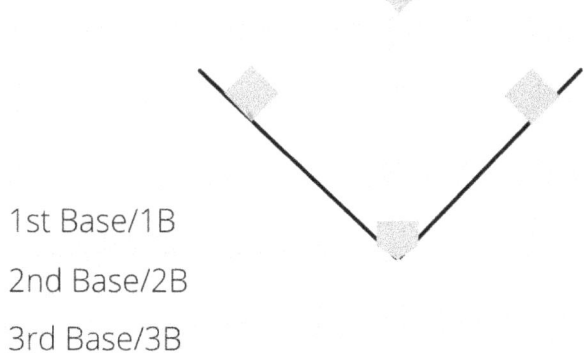

1st Base/1B

2nd Base/2B

3rd Base/3B

Home Plate/Home

Identify The Positions

Identify The Positions
Draw a line from the position name to the matching spot

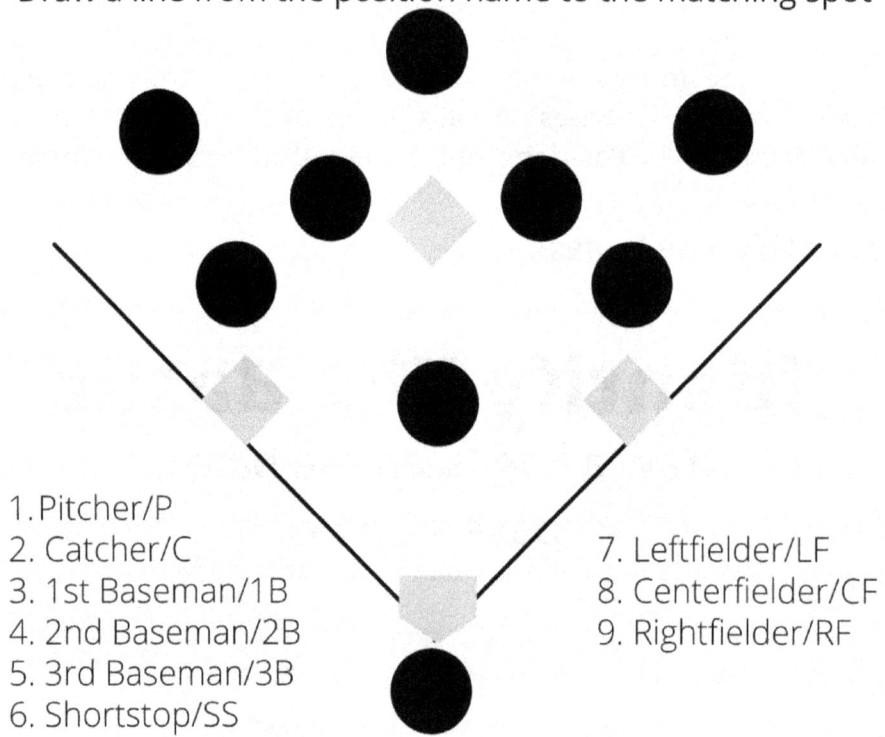

1. Pitcher/P
2. Catcher/C
3. 1st Baseman/1B
4. 2nd Baseman/2B
5. 3rd Baseman/3B
6. Shortstop/SS

7. Leftfielder/LF
8. Centerfielder/CF
9. Rightfielder/RF

Once your players know where the bases and positions are, their stress levels will decrease, and their performance will increase.

PRACTICE

Length

T-ball practice should be an hour long.

Defense And Baserunning

T-ball is a defensive and baserunning focused game. Since everyone makes contact, you have to make outs in the field. Since it's challenging to make outs in the field, being alert as a runner and running as fast as possible are significant advantages.

Coach Speeches (0 Minutes)

Spend zero time on team speeches. You'll have approximately 12 practices and eight games for a total of 20 events. Each event will be about 60 minutes long.

So, you have 1200 minutes of total improvement time in a season.

If you spend 5 minutes talking to the players at each event, that's 8% of your total time.

Giving the players 100 more minutes of practice time is more beneficial to their development than listening to 20 5-minute speeches.

Warm-Up (10 Minutes)

Start with three reps of "ready position." Hop into it like they will when they are older. Not too high, not too low. Hands out in front.

Next, work on running the bases. First, have one of your assistants run the bases while everyone watches. Then, have an assistant lead the players around the bases in a single file line. Next, have other assistants at each base, ensuring everyone touches the base. As the season progresses, get stricter about everyone touching every base. Then, toward the end of the season, make everyone do it again if anyone misses a base.

Then, have everyone run to first base and keep running through first base as if it's a close play. For t-ball players, running through first base is a difficult concept to grasp. So, work on running through first base during every practice, and eventually, the players will be doing it in the games.

Stations (3 Stations, 12 Minutes Each)

Break your team of 12 into three groups of 4.

Since t-ball is a defensive game, have two stations for defense and one for hitting.

Station #1

Fielding grounders

Have the four players spread out. Roll grounders toward them one at a time and have them throw it back to you. Try to get a good rhythm going so you can get a lot of reps in.

Have them scoop the ball instead of trap it. Nip that trapping thing some players do in the bud right away.

Defense Station #2

Throwing

Most players have limited experience throwing. The coach at this station should throw one or two out into an open field as an example. Then, have each player throw three balls out into an open area. Encourage the players to throw with better form each time. Once all players have thrown their three balls, have them all retrieve the balls simultaneously.

Repeat for 12 minutes.

Throwing into an open field is better than throwing into a fence. Let the players see the result of their efforts!

Hitting Station #3

Get four tees, one for each player.

Position the tees so that the hit balls go away from the other players.

Let each player hit three balls each and then have a "pause game" period where they go and retrieve the balls. If the players hit more than three balls at a time, retrieving the balls without help is difficult.

Remember, the first rule of t-ball is "let them put the ball on the tee themselves!"

The second rule of t-ball hitting is "swing as hard as possible!" Learning to swing hard is something best done at a young age. In t-ball, players get unlimited tries to hit, so attack the ball!

Also, stay out of the players' way when they are hitting. Some people will talk about angles while drawing lines in the dirt and positioning the players' feet. Avoid all of that.

In higher levels of baseball/softball, players have to hit a ball moving on both the vertical and horizontal plane. Therefore, it is a fool's errand to line up obsessively to hit a ball in a fixed spot. Instead, let the players be athletes and align themselves.

Kickball (13 Minutes)

Kickball is a lower-skilled version of t-ball. Kids love kickball. They will cheer when you announce that it's time to play kickball.

Divide the players up into two teams of six. Everyone plays the infield, including one pitcher's helper and one "player that stands on second base." You're the all-time pitcher, and ideally, you will do zero fielding. Let the pitcher's helper do that.

As the pitcher, try to use as much baseball lingo as possible. "Two outs, play's at second. Joey, you're backing up second." etc., between every pitch. Immerse them in the language. They will love it and learn at the same time.

Play with outs in kickball even if your league doesn't. It motivates the players to try harder, and it's better to get any "I've never been out before in my life" tantrums out of the way in a t-ball practice.

Play to 3 outs or whenever you get through the six-player lineup. Then switch sides. You should be able to get through each lineup once in the allotted time.

Breakdown (2 Minutes)

Get everyone to put their hands in the middle. You say "Panthers on 3. 1-2-3..." and then all the kids and coaches yell, "Panthers!" Practice the breakdown a couple of times during the first practice so that everyone gets it. This will be most players' first breakdown, so make sure everyone gets it right.

THE NIGHT BEFORE THE GAME

Batting Order

Bat in alphabetical order by first name. The players will be more likely to remember when it's their turn to bat, which makes the bench coaches' lives easier.

Rotate who bats first each game. Some leagues will bat everyone each inning, but players like to bat at the top of the order so they can run the bases each time during game situations. In leagues that bat everyone, after the last batter, the inning is over. The remaining players on the bases run around to home, but it's less exciting than live play.

Player Positions

Give all players equal chances to play each position. Also, rotate which position they play every inning. Even two innings in a row is too long to be in the outfield in t-ball.

Make up fake positions to have more infield spots than outfield spots. Left pitcher, right pitcher, and "the one that stands on second base" should get you enough.

Talkative Friends

Occasionally, certain players will talk to one another while overlooking the batter. Remember to place these social players on different sides of the field.

Dangerous Positions

"Pitcher" is more dangerous than other positions because it is close to the batter. Wait until later in the season to play less prepared players at "pitcher." If necessary, stand or kneel next to an unprepared pitcher and catch any line drives hit back at them.

First base is also a more dangerous position because players always throw the ball to first base. Most players will be unable to catch the ball on the fly, but many will be able to get their face out of harm's way. Only play prepared players at first base.

Lineup Card

The night before the game, make the lineup card with the batting order and positions by inning on an enormous piece of poster board. Then, take a picture of it and post it to the team app. The players will see it in the dugout, and every parent and coach will have a copy on their phone.

	1st Inning	2nd Inning	3rd Inning
Mildred	2nd	LCF	SS
Neville	LF	2nd	2B
Nolan	RCF	2B	RP
Oscar	CF	LP	LCF
Steve	2B	CF	3B
Cooper	RF	1B	LF
David	1B	RP	RF
Donald	LCF	3B	RCF
Earl	SS	LF	LP
Greg	LF	SS	CF
Jeremy	3B	RF	1B
John	RP	RCF	2nd

Opposing Coaches

Agree on the rules and modifications before the game. Even better, confirm the rules in an email or text the day before the game. If your game honors outs, then agree on that beforehand. If the game is "station to station" baserunning only, then decide ahead of time. Remember that hitting the ball off the tee is the primary accommodation. The rest of the game can be played like standard baseball, or at least with the rules of the next age group higher.

GAMEDAY

Pre-Game Warmup

Tell your team to get to the field 5 minutes before the game starts. Five and six-year-old performance starts high and degrades. Long warmups lead to poor performance.

Detailed Warmup List

1. Have the players hop into "ready position" 3 times.
2. Have the players run the bases once, or if the infield is unavailable, have them run 25 yards and back.

That's it. Now, the players are ready to play.

Coaching Guidelines

1. Always be dialed into the game. No coffee! No phone! Kids love playing for coaches who care!
2. Always let the players retrieve an overthrow! Never "slyly" stop a ball with your foot! It's disrespectful to the game!

Offense Coaching Responsibilities By Position

Home Plate

Retrieve the ball from wherever it ended up after the last play. Let the players on the other team throw it to you to allow them to practice throwing.

Then, hand the ball to the next player up to bat.

Let the players on your team put the ball on the tee themselves!

Putting the ball on the tee themselves both gives players confidence and makes it easier for them to align to the ball.

Again, putting the ball on the tee for a player is degrading! Let them do it themselves.

Play with only one ball!

Sometimes, coaches will take another ball out of their pocket after a foul ball. That's dangerous! The players go to field the foul ball and could get hit by the new ball.

Wait until the foul ball is retrieved and thrown back in. If the opposing coach tries to play with two balls when your team is fielding, scream "Time!", pause the game, and explain that you only want to play with one ball for safety.

First-Base Coach

The first base coach's responsibilities are to

1. Make sure the runner on first is paying attention before the batter swings.
2. Remind the runner on first base to run once the ball is hit.
3. Then, encourage the batter to run to/through first.

Third-Base Coach

As the third base coach, you should

1. Make sure both the runner on second and the runner on third are paying attention before the batter swings.
2. Once the ball is hit, encourage the runner on 3rd to run home.
3. Then, encourage the runner on 2nd base to run to 3rd.

Bench Coaches

The bench coaches' primary job is safety.

Rule #1

No bats in the dugout. Keep the bats outside the dugout.

Rule #2

No practice swings. Give the next player up his bat as he goes up to the plate.

Ideally, you will have two bench coaches.

One coach will stage the players to hit. The next player up and the one after that should have helmets on. Keep it moving. The less downtime, the more engaged the players will be.

The second coach will sit with the rest of the players and halt any dangerous activities.

The Transition From Offense To Defense

Once your team's time at bat is over, you need to get everyone out to the field in their correct position for that inning.

Some players will be able to use the lineup card to find their way to their position by themselves. Other players will need help.

You already sent out the lineup card to all parents and coaches the night before so that everyone will have it on their phone. Enlist as many coaches and parents as possible to get everyone to their position.

The faster everyone gets to their position, the better the team's performance will be for that inning.

Coaching Activities On Defense

When your team is fielding, concentrate on making sure the players closest to the ball are looking at the batter. When a good hitter is up to bat, "use your bullets" and encourage the kids to pay attention. Let players take a mental break when a poor hitter is up to bat.

If you have a good feel for where the batter will hit the ball, let the appropriate players know. They are more likely to listen to you if your recommendations are helpful, so only do this when confident. Skip this if it's hard for you to predict where the ball will be hit.

Infield Position Depth

Encourage each player to play at the proper depth. For example, the first and third baseman should play roughly as far from the batter as the base. "Let the ball come to you, and then step on the base!"

Same thing at shortstop and 2nd base. Have players stand far enough back so they can let the ball come to them and still have time to make a force out at second.

In t-ball, it is rare for a player to have the skill to make a play on the ball and then turn around and run back to a base for a force-out. If players are playing in front of the base, they usually take themselves out of the play before it starts.

Outfield Positioning

Make your outfielders play outfield! The outfielders should stand on the grass to allow the infielders to play without outfielder interference.

The centerfielder, in particular, will be able to make force outs at 2nd on hard-hit balls up the middle.

Encourage the other outfielders to play in the gaps between infielders. Then, they will have the opportunity to field balls and even make outs when the opposing team's base coaches are asleep at the wheel.

End Of Game Tunnel

Have all the coaches, parents, and fans of your team form a tunnel after the post-game handshake and have the players run through it. Cheer and say "great job" a lot. The players will love it.

Breakdown

Break it down at the end of the game.

PRACTICE EXPANSION

Alternate Practice Drills

As the season progresses and players improve on the basics, here are some alternate practice drills.

Force Play At Home

One player is the pitcher, and the other three players get in line at 3rd base.

Roll a grounder to the pitcher.

As you roll a grounder to the pitcher, the runner at 3rd runs for home.

The pitcher fields the ball and runs home to make the force out.

Each player fields three times, once for each runner. Then, rotate.

Force Play At First

This drill is the same setup as "force play at home" but with the runners starting at home and the fielder playing 1st base. Since the 1st baseman is closer to first than the pitcher is to home, this should be easier for the fielder.

Learn To Tag

Show the players at the station how to tag. Show all the different scenarios.

1. Ball in glove + tag with glove = out
2. Ball in hand + tag with hand = out
3. Ball in glove + tag with hand = safe
4. Ball in hand + tag with glove = safe

Have each player tag you standing still.

Then roll the ball to each player and have them tag you as you run to a base.

Catching The Ball

Get a tennis ball and have the four kids in your station spread out. Throw a soft toss to each kid one at a time. Almost all the players will start with an underhand basket catch. In the beginning, it's the coach's responsibility to throw the ball so it's easy for the player to catch it. As the players get better, the coach can increase the difficulty by throwing from a longer distance, intentionally throwing it slightly off target, and encouraging them to catch in a more advanced way than the basket catch.

"Two Hands!"

Many coaches and parents will encourage the players to catch with two hands. However, while two hands can be an appropriate learning step, in the long run, catching the ball with one hand is the default.

It's easier to catch and easier to throw quickly if a player catches with one hand.

If a player has the skill to catch with one hand, or even if that skill is emerging, leave that player alone!

Expand Your Range

Once players are good at fielding ground balls hit directly at them, encourage them to take one shuffle step toward where the ball is hit. It's almost the same drill as the standard fielding grounders station. The modification is that the coach rolls the ball one shuffle away from the player.

Most t-ball players can only field a ball hit directly at them. A player that can shuffle once and field a ball will have a defensive range three times bigger than the average player.

Soft Toss/Batting Cages

If your team is hitting well, use the last few practices to hit without the tee. Make it easy by throwing the ball where the player's bat will be, and encourage the players to keep swinging as hard as possible! Feel free to throw underhand.

Intrasquad Scrimmage

As the season goes on, your team may separate in skill from many opponents. Running an intrasquad scrimmage instead of a practice one week is an excellent way to get your players some good competition against energized opponents. Split the players into two equal teams of six and position players in the infield only. The intrasquad scrimmage may be the highest level game you play all year.

MISCELLANEOUS ISSUES

Left-Handed Hitters

Left-handed hitters can get discouraged in t-ball because their good hits go right to the 1st baseman, and the 1st baseman is more likely to get them out. So, they try to hit it to the third-base side or try to hit the ball less hard. Encourage them to hit it as hard as possible. If their natural swing sends the ball to the right side of the field, that's ok. Let them know that eventually, they will be hitting home runs if they swing hard. So, swing as hard as possible!

Good Hitters

Good hitters of all types can have a similar problem as lefties in t-ball. They hit the ball up the middle with power, only to have someone pick up the ball and stand on second for a force out of the runner on first. Explain that hard-hit balls up the middle are great! Soon, those will carry into center field and then over the fence.

Hot Weather

Games are often scheduled for mid-day on the weekends. When it's hot, performance will suffer.

Keep performance as high as possible by

    1. Having the players get to the field only 5 minutes before

the game starts. Note: this should be the standard arrival time for all games.
2. Having the players sit in the shade while waiting to go up to bat. Find a shady place a little bit farther away from where they would "normally" sit if necessary. You should have two bench coaches, and they will be able to deal with the logistics of having a long walk from wherever shade is to the plate.
3. Send an email out to the parents to encourage their players to drink water before showing up to the game.
4. Drink water during the game in the dugout.

Fans

Try to encourage a big fan turnout. Tell the parents to let their player's teachers know when the games are. Often, a teacher will have multiple students playing in the same game, so they get extra bang for their buck when attending a game.

VICTORY!

End Of Season Party

After you have done a great job coaching, everyone will want to have an end-of-season party. Feel free to let someone else plan the party. One of the goals of coaching is to have as many players as possible sign up for the next season, and a party can encourage future interest.

ABOUT THE AUTHOR

Jerry Baseball

Jerry Baseball has spent his life analyzing and optimizing his way to victory. He is pleased to have shared his t-ball coaching template with you. He hopes that everyone enjoys coaching t-ball as much as he does.

jerrybaseball4@gmail.com

COACHING YOUTH BASEBALL

Coaching T-Ball: Organize And Optimize Your Way To A Great Season

Coaching Machine Pitch: Organize And Optimize Your Way To A Great Season

www.ingramcontent.com/pod-product-compliance
Lightning Source LLC
Chambersburg PA
CBHW071314060426
42444CB00035B/2612